Stewart, John
    Elephant school. – Working animals series)
    1. Elephants – Juvenile literature
    I. Title   II. Series
    636'.961   QL737.P98

    ISBN 0–7136–2814–6

A & C Black (Publishers) Limited
35 Bedford Row, London WC1R 4JH

Filmset by August Filmsetting, Haydock, St. Helens
Printed in Hong Kong by Dai Nippon Printing Co. Ltd

Elephant

John Stewart

A & C Black · London

This is the entrance to a very special school. It's a school for elephants in the forests of Northern Thailand.

The elephants who live here are learning to work in the forest. Their job is to drag heavy logs of teak wood through the forest to the nearest road. Then lorries will take the wood to factories. It will be made into boats, or furniture.

Somchai and his friend Chan have just arrived at the school. They have come to learn how to work with the elephants. The head of the school shows them around.

This is the elephants' classroom. It's a big open space where all the trees have been cleared away.

The men who work with elephants are called mahouts. Each man has his own elephant.

Soon, Somchai and Chan will each have their own elephant to train. Until then, they are helping to look after some of the mother elephants and their young.

The baby elephants are called calves. They are too young to be trained, so they watch the older elephants at work.

Somchai and Chan make sure that the calves don't get into trouble.

One morning a lorry comes to the school. Inside are two young elephants, one for Somchai and one for Chan.

This is Somchai's elephant. She's a female called Pang Pon. Chan's elephant is a male called Plai Lua. They are only six years old, so they aren't very big.

Somchai gives the elephants some tasty bamboo
shoots and a long cool bath.

Soon the elephants have got used to their new home and it's time to start lessons.

Somchai and Chan and some of the older mahouts gather round Pang Pon. They talk quietly to her and slip a rope over her head.

The men pull Pang Pon into a small pen made of wood. This is where she will have her first lessons. Pang Pon isn't hurt but she is frightened. She trumpets loudly and digs her feet into the ground.

After a time, Pang Pon calms down and stands quietly in her pen. Somchai gives her some bamboo shoots as a reward. He hides a bannana under his shirt and Pang Pon soon finds it.

Every day, Pang Pon has lessons in her pen. She learns to understand commands like 'Down' and 'Stand still'. Somchai teaches her to bend her knee when he prods her foot with a stick. He always gives her a reward when she learns well.

After a few weeks, Somchai and Pang Pon are firm friends.

Somchai decides that he is ready to sit on Pang Pon's back for the first time. He tells Pang Pon to bend her knee and make a step for him to climb on.

Very gently, Somchai lowers himself on to Pang Pon's back. He doesn't want to frighten her. But now Pang Pon is used to him. She gives a little shake and then stands still and quiet.

Soon, Pang Pon is ready to have lessons with the other elephants.

Every morning, before lessons, the mahouts give their elephants a wash. Elephants like to squirt mud and dust over their backs. This protects them from the sun, but it makes them very dirty. Somchai and Chan brush off all the mud and dust.

14

Then the elephants have a bath. They wallow in the cool water. The mahouts scrub their elephants until they are shiny and clean.

When everyone is ready, the class lines up for inspection. The head of the school checks that all the elephants are fit and well.

Lessons start very early in the morning. Here, Pang Pon and her class are learning how to help the mahouts climb on to their backs. Can you see how they do this?

While they are working Somchai talks to Pang Pon. If she behaves badly, Somchai scolds her and tells her that she's being silly. If she does well he tells her she's a clever girl and gives her a reward.

Pang Pon soon learns to understand the words
'Lie down'. She will lie on her side as if she is
asleep. This means that the vet can check her skin
for cuts and snake bites or give her an injection.

Next Pang Pon must learn to get dressed. The elephants wear wooden saddles with chains for dragging logs. They must stand very still while they are being dressed. Some of the older animals even help their mahouts with the heavy equipment.

Pang Pon learns by watching the older elephants.
These male elephants can lift heavy logs and hold
them between their tusks and trunk.

Pang Pon can't do this. She's a female elephant
so she doesn't have any tusks. But she learns to
lift up a log with her trunk or push it with her head.

Somchai sits on Pang Pon's back. When he prods
her with his toes or with his stick, she learns which
way he wants to go and what he wants her to do.

Soon Pang Pon can drag logs behind her like the older elephants. She and Somchai practise over and over again until they both know what to do. Chan and his elephant practise with them. They are learning to work as a team.

The young elephants learn new things every day.
Here is one of Pang Pon's class learning how to
balance on a log. This will help the elephants to
walk along the steep, narrow forest paths where
tractors cannot go.

Pang Pon and Somchai don't work all the time.
Lessons stop at mid-day and Pang Pon goes into the
forest to look for bamboo shoots or leaves to eat.
Somchai will go and fetch her for school the next day.

Pang Pon and Somchai will spend four years at the elephant school. Pang Pon will learn to stack logs into piles and load them on to lorries. She'll learn to work in a team and do lots of different jobs. She'll be much more useful than a tractor and she won't cost so much to keep.

Pang Pon and Somchai will always work together. When they are old, they will retire together, but that's another story.

More about working elephants

For thousands of years, elephants have been used as working animals. We have used elephants for carrying heavy loads, in religious and ceremonial processions and even, in war, for attacking foot soldiers. Only Asiatic elephants are used as working animals. The larger African elephants are thought to be less intelligent and impossible to train.

The Young Elephant Training Centre was set up in 1969. It is part of the Forest Industry Organisation in Thailand, which owns about 100 elephants. Elephants at the Centre are trained to work in the teak forests of Thailand. When the teak trees have been cut down, the elephants drag the heavy logs out of the forest to the nearest road. From there, the logs are carried by lorry to the sawmills.

Unlike tractors, elephants don't need petrol and they don't cause pollution. They do need a lot of food, though. A fully grown elephant eats over 200 kg of leaves and plants, and drinks over 200 litres of water each day.

In the past, wild elephants were captured for training, but nowadays working elephants are born in captivity. The new-born elephant weights about 90 kg and is about 60 cm tall. For the first two years, it stays with its mother. Then it spends three or four years in the forest, watching the older elephants at work. When it is six years old, the elephant will go to the Centre. The elephants at the Centre have a three month holiday from March until May, when it is too hot to work.

After four years training, the elephant will be ready to start work in the forest with its mahout. When it is sixty years old, the elephant can retire. It will roam the forest with a mahout to take care of it. Elephants usually live for about seventy years.